MY BRIEF 4-YEAR JOURNAL

MY BRIEF 4-YEAR JOURNAL

For information address:
Dr. Percival G. Ricketts, LMHC, PA
10031 Pines Boulevard, Suite 242
Pembroke Pines, FL 33024

ISBN - 13: 978-0-692-15192-1

Printed in the USA

Date Started: _____

Date Completed: _____

These are my private thoughts. Please do not read them.

If this journal is found, please return it to the owner at the

 following address:

Name:_____

Street Address:_____

City:_____

State: _____**Zip Code:**_____

Telephone: (**) -**   **-**   **.**

Don't try to remember it.

Write it down!

Using Your Brief 4-Year Journal

Journaling is a very effective therapeutic tool that many individuals find useful. This volume, is a brief, ruled, guided journal with simple and useful reminders. It is designed to help you record highlights of each day for 4 years from the day that you started (regardless of when that is). It is ideal for students from high school through college and even through adulthood. The practice of recording your daily highlights can be beneficial from many standpoints. It prevents you from relying on your memory, which is sometimes unreliable. It can be used to keep you abreast of important life changes and trends including personal thoughts, feelings and behaviors. Finally, it can help you check your progress to ensure that you are on track with your goals, and it can give you the opportunity to look back periodically and see from how far you have come.

A hand-written journal is very important. Perhaps, even more than the notes than you write on your mobile phone or tablet. You could write in secret codes that only you can understand, and you don't have to worry about anyone hacking into it. Unless you personally delete data that you entered, you will not lose any information either. You will also never need power to use it, nor will ever have to charge or recharge anything. You will never have to worry about cracked screens or frozen data while you are using your journal, and it fits nicely into handbags and backpacks and pouches. You can take it with you wherever you go. Keeping a brief journal is simply a great idea.

Choose a specific time each night to write in your journal. Write only one or two brief sentences that capture the highlights of your day. Then, at the end of each week, write a summary of the most important thing that you would like to remember about that week.

May the next 4 years be some of your most memorable.

Daily Highlights

Sunday_____
_____
_____
_____

Monday_____
_____
_____
_____

Tuesday_____
_____
_____
_____

Wednesday_____
_____
_____
_____

Thursday_____
_____
_____
_____

Friday_____
_____
_____
_____

Saturday_____
_____
_____
_____

What I would like to remember about this week

_____
_____
_____
_____
_____
_____
_____

Week Beginning: _____

Daily Highlights

Sunday_____
_____
_____
_____

Monday_____
_____
_____
_____

Tuesday_____
_____
_____
_____

Wednesday_____
_____
_____
_____

Thursday_____
_____
_____
_____

Friday_____
_____
_____
_____

Saturday_____
_____
_____
_____

What I would like to remember about this week

_____
_____
_____
_____
_____
_____
_____
_____

Week Beginning: _____

Daily Highlights

Sunday_____

_____

_____

_____

Monday_____

_____

_____

_____

Tuesday_____

_____

_____

_____

Wednesday_____

_____

_____

_____

Thursday_____

_____

_____

_____

Friday_____

_____

_____

_____

Saturday_____

_____

_____

_____

What I would like to remember about this week

_____

_____

_____

_____

_____

_____

_____

Laugh

Week Beginning: _____

Daily Highlights

nday_____
_____
_____
_____

onday_____
_____
_____
_____

esday_____
_____
_____
_____

ednesday_____
_____
_____
_____

ursday_____
_____
_____
_____

iday_____
_____
_____
_____

aturday_____
_____
_____
_____

What I would like to remember about this week

_____
_____
_____
_____
_____
_____
_____

Week Beginning: _____

Daily Highlights

Sunday_____
_____
_____
_____

Monday_____
_____
_____
_____

Tuesday_____
_____
_____
_____

Wednesday_____
_____
_____
_____

Thursday_____
_____
_____
_____

Friday_____
_____
_____
_____

Saturday_____
_____
_____
_____

What I would like to remember about this week

_____
_____
_____
_____
_____
_____
_____

Week Beginning: _____

Daily Highlights

Sunday _____
_____
_____
_____

Monday _____
_____
_____
_____

Tuesday _____
_____
_____
_____

Wednesday _____
_____
_____
_____

Thursday _____
_____
_____
_____

Friday _____
_____
_____
_____

Saturday _____
_____
_____
_____

What I would like to remember about this week

_____
_____
_____
_____
_____
_____
_____

Daily Highlights

Sunday_____
_____
_____
_____

Monday_____
_____
_____
_____

Tuesday_____
_____
_____
_____

Wednesday_____
_____
_____
_____

Thursday_____
_____
_____
_____

Friday_____
_____
_____
_____

Saturday_____
_____
_____
_____

What I would like to remember about this week

_____
_____
_____
_____
_____
_____
_____

Rest

Daily Highlights

Sunday_____
_____
_____
_____

Monday_____
_____
_____
_____

Tuesday_____
_____
_____
_____

Wednesday_____
_____
_____
_____

Thursday_____
_____
_____
_____

Friday_____
_____
_____
_____

Saturday_____
_____
_____
_____

What I would like to remember about this week

_____
_____
_____
_____
_____
_____
_____
_____

Week Beginning: _____

Daily Highlights

nday_____
_____
_____
_____

onday_____
_____
_____
_____

esday_____
_____
_____
_____

ednesday_____
_____
_____
_____

ursday_____
_____
_____
_____

iday_____
_____
_____

aturday_____
_____
_____
_____

What I would like to remember about this week

_____
_____
_____
_____
_____
_____
_____
_____

Week Beginning: _____

Daily Highlights

Sunday_____
_____
_____
_____

Monday_____
_____
_____
_____

Tuesday_____
_____
_____
_____

Wednesday_____
_____
_____
_____

Thursday_____
_____
_____
_____

Friday_____
_____
_____
_____

Saturday_____
_____
_____
_____

What I would like to remember about this week

_____
_____
_____
_____
_____
_____
_____
_____

Daily Highlights

Sunday_____
_____
_____
_____

Monday_____
_____
_____
_____

Tuesday_____
_____
_____
_____

Wednesday_____
_____
_____
_____

Thursday_____
_____
_____
_____

Friday_____
_____
_____
_____

Saturday_____
_____
_____
_____

What I would like to remember about this week

_____
_____
_____
_____
_____
_____
_____

Be kind to others

Daily Highlights

Sunday_____
_____
_____
_____

Monday_____
_____
_____
_____

Tuesday_____
_____
_____
_____

Wednesday_____
_____
_____
_____

Thursday_____
_____
_____
_____

Friday_____
_____
_____
_____

Saturday_____
_____
_____
_____

What I would like to remember about this week

_____
_____
_____
_____
_____
_____
_____

Daily Highlights

Sunday_____
_____
_____
_____

Monday_____
_____
_____
_____

Tuesday_____
_____
_____
_____

Wednesday_____
_____
_____
_____

Thursday_____
_____
_____
_____

Friday_____
_____
_____
_____

Saturday_____
_____
_____
_____

What I would like to remember about this week

_____
_____
_____
_____
_____
_____
_____
_____

Week Beginning: _____

Daily Highlights

nday_____
_____
_____
_____

onday_____
_____
_____
_____

esday_____
_____
_____
_____

ednesday_____
_____
_____
_____

ursday_____
_____
_____
_____

iday_____
_____
_____

aturday_____
_____
_____

What I would like to remember about this week

_____
_____
_____
_____
_____
_____

Daily Highlights

Sunday_____
_____
_____
_____

Monday_____
_____
_____
_____

Tuesday_____
_____
_____
_____

Wednesday_____
_____
_____
_____

Thursday_____
_____
_____
_____

Friday_____
_____
_____
_____

Saturday_____
_____
_____
_____

What I would like to remember about this week

_____
_____
_____
_____
_____
_____
_____

Learn to meditate

Week Beginning: _____

Daily Highlights

Sunday_____
_____
_____
_____

Monday_____
_____
_____
_____

Tuesday_____
_____
_____
_____

Wednesday_____
_____
_____
_____

Thursday_____
_____
_____
_____

Friday_____
_____
_____
_____

Saturday_____
_____
_____
_____

What I would like to remember about this week

_____
_____
_____
_____
_____
_____
_____
_____

Week Beginning: _____

Daily Highlights

Sunday_____
_____
_____
_____

Monday_____
_____
_____
_____

Tuesday_____
_____
_____
_____

Wednesday_____
_____
_____
_____

Thursday_____
_____
_____
_____

Friday_____
_____
_____
_____

Saturday_____
_____
_____
_____

What I would like to remember about this week

_____
_____
_____
_____
_____
_____
_____

Week Beginning: _____

Daily Highlights

Sunday_____
_____
_____
_____

Monday_____
_____
_____
_____

Tuesday_____
_____
_____
_____

Wednesday_____
_____
_____
_____

Thursday_____
_____
_____
_____

Friday_____
_____
_____
_____

Saturday_____
_____
_____
_____

What I would like to remember about this week

_____
_____
_____
_____
_____
_____
_____
_____

Smile

Daily Highlights

Sunday_____
_____
_____
_____

Monday_____
_____
_____
_____

Tuesday_____
_____
_____
_____

Wednesday_____
_____
_____
_____

Thursday_____
_____
_____
_____

Friday_____
_____
_____
_____

Saturday_____
_____
_____
_____

What I would like to remember about this week

_____
_____
_____
_____
_____
_____
_____
_____

Week Beginning: _____

Daily Highlights

Sunday_____

Monday_____

Tuesday_____

Wednesday_____

Thursday_____

Friday_____

Saturday_____

What I would like to remember about this week

31

Daily Highlights

Sunday_____
_____
_____
_____

Monday_____
_____
_____
_____

Tuesday_____
_____
_____
_____

Wednesday_____
_____
_____
_____

Thursday_____
_____
_____
_____

Friday_____
_____
_____
_____

Saturday_____
_____
_____
_____

What I would like to remember about this week

_____
_____
_____
_____
_____
_____
_____
_____

Week Beginning: _____

Daily Highlights

Sunday_____
_____
_____
_____

Monday_____
_____
_____
_____

Tuesday_____
_____
_____
_____

Wednesday_____
_____
_____
_____

Thursday_____
_____
_____
_____

Friday_____
_____
_____

Saturday_____
_____
_____
_____

What I would like to remember about this week

_____
_____
_____
_____
_____
_____
_____

Daily Highlights

Sunday_____

_____

_____

_____

Monday_____

_____

_____

_____

Tuesday_____

_____

_____

_____

Wednesday_____

_____

_____

_____

Thursday_____

_____

_____

_____

Friday_____

_____

_____

_____

Saturday_____

_____

_____

_____

What I would like to remember about this week

_____

_____

_____

_____

_____

_____

_____

Do something nice for someone

Daily Highlights

Sunday_____
_____
_____
_____

Monday_____
_____
_____
_____

Tuesday_____
_____
_____
_____

Wednesday_____
_____
_____
_____

Thursday_____
_____
_____
_____

Friday_____
_____
_____
_____

Saturday_____
_____
_____
_____

What I would like to remember about this week

_____
_____
_____
_____
_____
_____
_____
_____

Week Beginning: _____

Daily Highlights

Sunday_____
_____
_____
_____

Monday_____
_____
_____
_____

Tuesday_____
_____
_____
_____

Wednesday_____
_____
_____
_____

Thursday_____
_____
_____
_____

Friday_____
_____
_____
_____

Saturday_____
_____
_____
_____

What I would like to remember about this week

_____
_____
_____
_____
_____
_____
_____

Daily Highlights

Sunday_____
_____
_____
_____

Monday_____
_____
_____
_____

Tuesday_____
_____
_____
_____

Wednesday_____
_____
_____
_____

Thursday_____
_____
_____
_____

Friday_____
_____
_____
_____

Saturday_____
_____
_____
_____

What I would like to remember about this week

_____
_____
_____
_____
_____
_____
_____
_____

Week Beginning: _____

Daily Highlights

Sunday_____
_____
_____
_____

Monday_____
_____
_____
_____

Tuesday_____
_____
_____
_____

Wednesday_____
_____
_____
_____

Thursday_____
_____
_____
_____

Friday_____
_____
_____
_____

Saturday_____
_____
_____
_____

What I would like to remember about this week

_____
_____
_____
_____
_____
_____
_____

Take a break from your phone.

Don't call. Don't text. Don't check any e-mails

Week Beginning: _____

Daily Highlights

Sunday_____
_____
_____
_____

Monday_____
_____
_____
_____

Tuesday_____
_____
_____
_____

Wednesday_____
_____
_____
_____

Thursday_____
_____
_____
_____

Friday_____
_____
_____
_____

Saturday_____
_____
_____
_____

What I would like to remember about this week

_____
_____
_____
_____
_____
_____
_____

41

Week Beginning: _____

Daily Highlights

Sunday_____
_____
_____
_____

Monday_____
_____
_____
_____

Tuesday_____
_____
_____
_____

Wednesday_____
_____
_____
_____

Thursday_____
_____
_____
_____

Friday_____
_____
_____
_____

Saturday_____
_____
_____
_____

What I would like to remember about this week

_____
_____
_____
_____
_____
_____
_____
_____

Daily Highlights

Sunday_____
_____
_____
_____

Monday_____
_____
_____
_____

Tuesday_____
_____
_____
_____

Wednesday_____
_____
_____
_____

Thursday_____
_____
_____
_____

Friday_____
_____
_____
_____

Saturday_____
_____
_____
_____

What I would like to remember about this week

_____
_____
_____
_____
_____
_____
_____

Daily Highlights

Sunday_____

_____

_____

_____

Monday_____

_____

_____

_____

Tuesday_____

_____

_____

_____

Wednesday_____

_____

_____

_____

Thursday_____

_____

_____

_____

Friday_____

_____

_____

_____

Saturday_____

_____

_____

_____

What I would like to remember about this week

_____

_____

_____

_____

_____

_____

_____

_____

Before you give up, try harder.

Daily Highlights

Sunday_____
_____
_____
_____

Monday_____
_____
_____
_____

Tuesday_____
_____
_____
_____

Wednesday_____
_____
_____
_____

Thursday_____
_____
_____
_____

Friday_____
_____
_____
_____

Saturday_____
_____
_____
_____

What I would like to remember about this week

_____
_____
_____
_____
_____
_____
_____
_____

Week Beginning: _____

Daily Highlights

nday_____
_____
_____
_____

onday_____
_____
_____
_____

esday_____
_____
_____
_____

ednesday_____
_____
_____
_____

ursday_____
_____
_____
_____

iday_____
_____
_____
_____

aturday_____
_____
_____
_____

What I would like to remember about this week

_____
_____
_____
_____
_____
_____
_____
_____

Daily Highlights

Sunday_____

_____

_____

_____

Monday_____

_____

_____

_____

Tuesday_____

_____

_____

_____

Wednesday_____

_____

_____

_____

Thursday_____

_____

_____

_____

Friday_____

_____

_____

_____

Saturday_____

_____

_____

_____

What I would like to remember about this week

_____

_____

_____

_____

_____

_____

_____

_____

Week Beginning: _____

Daily Highlights

Sunday_____
_____
_____
_____

Monday_____
_____
_____
_____

Tuesday_____
_____
_____
_____

Wednesday_____
_____
_____
_____

Thursday_____
_____
_____
_____

Friday_____
_____
_____

Saturday_____
_____
_____
_____

What I would like to remember about this week

_____
_____
_____
_____
_____
_____
_____

Say hello to someone

Week Beginning: _____

Daily Highlights

Sunday_____
_____
_____
_____

Monday_____
_____
_____
_____

Tuesday_____
_____
_____
_____

Wednesday_____
_____
_____
_____

Thursday_____
_____
_____
_____

Friday_____
_____
_____
_____

Saturday_____
_____
_____
_____

What I would like to remember about this week

_____
_____
_____
_____
_____
_____
_____

Listen

Daily Highlights

nday_____
_____
_____
_____

onday_____
_____
_____
_____

esday_____
_____
_____
_____

ednesday_____
_____
_____
_____

ursday_____
_____
_____
_____

iday_____
_____
_____
_____

aturday_____
_____
_____
_____

What I would like to remember about this week

_____
_____
_____
_____
_____
_____
_____

Daily Highlights

Sunday_____
_____
_____
_____

Monday_____
_____
_____
_____

Tuesday_____
_____
_____
_____

Wednesday_____
_____
_____
_____

Thursday_____
_____
_____
_____

Friday_____
_____
_____
_____

Saturday_____
_____
_____
_____

What I would like to remember about this week

_____
_____
_____
_____
_____
_____
_____

Week Beginning: _____

Daily Highlights

Sunday_____

_____

_____

_____

Monday_____

_____

_____

_____

Tuesday_____

_____

_____

_____

Wednesday_____

_____

_____

_____

Thursday_____

_____

_____

_____

Friday_____

_____

_____

_____

Saturday_____

_____

_____

_____

What I would like to remember about this week

_____

_____

_____

_____

_____

_____

_____

_____

Daily Highlights

Sunday _____
_____
_____
_____

Monday _____
_____
_____
_____

Tuesday _____
_____
_____
_____

Wednesday _____
_____
_____
_____

Thursday _____
_____
_____
_____

Friday _____
_____
_____
_____

Saturday _____
_____
_____
_____

What I would like to remember about this week

_____
_____
_____
_____
_____
_____
_____
_____

Give someone a compliment

Daily Highlights

Sunday_____
_____
_____
_____

Monday_____
_____
_____
_____

Tuesday_____
_____
_____
_____

Wednesday_____
_____
_____
_____

Thursday_____
_____
_____
_____

Friday_____
_____
_____
_____

Saturday_____
_____
_____
_____

What I would like to remember about this week

_____
_____
_____
_____
_____
_____
_____

Daily Highlights

nday_____
_____
_____
_____

onday_____
_____
_____
_____

esday_____
_____
_____
_____

ednesday_____
_____
_____
_____

ursday_____
_____
_____
_____

iday_____
_____
_____
_____

aturday_____
_____
_____
_____

What I would like to remember about this week

_____
_____
_____
_____
_____
_____
_____

Relax

Daily Highlights

Sunday_____
_____
_____
_____

Monday_____
_____
_____
_____

Tuesday_____
_____
_____
_____

Wednesday_____
_____
_____
_____

Thursday_____
_____
_____
_____

Friday_____
_____
_____
_____

Saturday_____
_____
_____
_____

What I would like to remember about this week

_____
_____
_____
_____
_____
_____
_____
_____

Daily Highlights

Sunday_____
_____
_____
_____

Monday_____
_____
_____
_____

Tuesday_____
_____
_____
_____

Wednesday_____
_____
_____
_____

Thursday_____
_____
_____
_____

Friday_____
_____
_____
_____

Saturday_____
_____
_____
_____

What I would like to remember about this week

_____
_____
_____
_____
_____
_____
_____
_____

Week Beginning: _____

Daily Highlights

Sunday_____

_____

_____

_____

Monday_____

_____

_____

_____

Tuesday_____

_____

_____

_____

Wednesday_____

_____

_____

_____

Thursday_____

_____

_____

_____

Friday_____

_____

_____

_____

Saturday_____

_____

_____

_____

What I would like to remember about this week

_____

_____

_____

_____

_____

_____

_____

63

Daily Highlights

Sunday_____

_____

_____

_____

Monday_____

_____

_____

_____

Tuesday_____

_____

_____

_____

Wednesday_____

_____

_____

_____

Thursday_____

_____

_____

_____

Friday_____

_____

_____

_____

Saturday_____

_____

_____

_____

What I would like to remember about this week

_____

_____

_____

_____

_____

_____

_____

Say "thank you."

Week Beginning: _____

Daily Highlights

Sunday_____
_____
_____
_____

Monday_____
_____
_____
_____

Tuesday_____
_____
_____
_____

Wednesday_____
_____
_____
_____

Thursday_____
_____
_____
_____

Friday_____
_____
_____
_____

Saturday_____
_____
_____
_____

What I would like to remember about this week

_____
_____
_____
_____
_____
_____
_____
_____

Week Beginning: _____

Daily Highlights

Sunday_____

_____

_____

_____

Monday_____

_____

_____

_____

Tuesday_____

_____

_____

_____

Wednesday_____

_____

_____

_____

Thursday_____

_____

_____

_____

Friday_____

_____

_____

_____

Saturday_____

_____

_____

_____

What I would like to remember about this week

_____

_____

_____

_____

_____

_____

_____

Daily Highlights

Sunday_____
_____
_____
_____

Monday_____
_____
_____
_____

Tuesday_____
_____
_____
_____

Wednesday_____
_____
_____
_____

Thursday_____
_____
_____
_____

Friday_____
_____
_____
_____

Saturday_____
_____
_____
_____

What I would like to remember about this week

_____
_____
_____
_____
_____
_____
_____
_____

Monitor your health.

Get a check-up.

Daily Highlights

Sunday_____
_____
_____
_____

Monday_____
_____
_____
_____

Tuesday_____
_____
_____
_____

Wednesday_____
_____
_____
_____

Thursday_____
_____
_____
_____

Friday_____
_____
_____
_____

Saturday_____
_____
_____
_____

What I would like to remember about this week

_____
_____
_____
_____
_____
_____
_____
_____

Think before you act.

Week Beginning: _____

Daily Highlights

Sunday_____
_____
_____
_____

Monday_____
_____
_____
_____

Tuesday_____
_____
_____
_____

Wednesday_____
_____
_____
_____

Thursday_____
_____
_____
_____

Friday_____
_____
_____
_____

Saturday_____
_____
_____
_____

What I would like to remember about this week

_____
_____
_____
_____
_____
_____
_____

Daily Highlights

Sunday_____
_____
_____
_____

Monday_____
_____
_____
_____

Tuesday_____
_____
_____
_____

Wednesday_____
_____
_____
_____

Thursday_____
_____
_____
_____

Friday_____
_____
_____
_____

Saturday_____
_____
_____
_____

What I would like to remember about this week

_____
_____
_____
_____
_____
_____
_____
_____

Daily Highlights

Sunday_____

_____

_____

_____

Monday_____

_____

_____

_____

Tuesday_____

_____

_____

_____

Wednesday_____

_____

_____

_____

Thursday_____

_____

_____

_____

Friday_____

_____

_____

_____

Saturday_____

_____

_____

_____

What I would like to remember about this week

_____

_____

_____

_____

_____

_____

_____

_____

Daily Highlights

Sunday _____
_____
_____
_____

Monday _____
_____
_____
_____

Tuesday _____
_____
_____
_____

Wednesday _____
_____
_____
_____

Thursday _____
_____
_____
_____

Friday _____
_____
_____
_____

Saturday _____
_____
_____
_____

What I would like to remember about this week

_____
_____
_____
_____
_____
_____
_____
_____

Believe in yourself and your abilities.

You can do it!

Week Beginning: _____

Daily Highlights

nday_____
_____
_____
_____

onday_____
_____
_____
_____

esday_____
_____
_____
_____

ednesday_____
_____
_____
_____

ursday_____
_____
_____
_____

iday_____
_____
_____
_____

aturday_____
_____
_____
_____

What I would like to remember about this week

_____
_____
_____
_____
_____
_____
_____
_____

Daily Highlights

Sunday_____

_____

_____

_____

Monday_____

_____

_____

_____

Tuesday_____

_____

_____

_____

Wednesday_____

_____

_____

_____

Thursday_____

_____

_____

_____

Friday_____

_____

_____

_____

Saturday_____

_____

_____

_____

What I would like to remember about this week

_____

_____

_____

_____

_____

_____

_____

_____

Help someone.

Daily Highlights

Sunday_____
_____
_____
_____

Monday_____
_____
_____
_____

Tuesday_____
_____
_____
_____

Wednesday_____
_____
_____
_____

Thursday_____
_____
_____
_____

Friday_____
_____
_____
_____

Saturday_____
_____
_____
_____

What I would like to remember about this week

_____
_____
_____
_____
_____
_____
_____

Daily Highlights

Sunday_____
_____
_____
_____

Monday_____
_____
_____
_____

Tuesday_____
_____
_____
_____

Wednesday_____
_____
_____
_____

Thursday_____
_____
_____
_____

Friday_____
_____
_____
_____

Saturday_____
_____
_____
_____

What I would like to remember about this week

_____
_____
_____
_____
_____
_____
_____

Show someone you care

Week Beginning: _____

Daily Highlights

nday_____

_____

_____

_____

onday_____

_____

_____

_____

esday_____

_____

_____

_____

ednesday_____

_____

_____

_____

ursday_____

_____

_____

_____

iday_____

_____

_____

_____

aturday_____

_____

_____

_____

What I would like to remember about this week

_____

_____

_____

_____

_____

_____

_____

_____

Week Beginning: _____

Daily Highlights

Sunday_____

_____

_____

_____

Monday_____

_____

_____

_____

Tuesday_____

_____

_____

_____

Wednesday_____

_____

_____

_____

Thursday_____

_____

_____

_____

Friday_____

_____

_____

_____

Saturday_____

_____

_____

_____

What I would like to remember about this week

_____

_____

_____

_____

_____

_____

_____

_____

Week Beginning: _____

Daily Highlights

Sunday_____
_____
_____
_____

Monday_____
_____
_____
_____

Tuesday_____
_____
_____
_____

Wednesday_____
_____
_____
_____

Thursday_____
_____
_____
_____

Friday_____
_____
_____
_____

Saturday_____
_____
_____
_____

What I would like to remember about this week

_____
_____
_____
_____
_____
_____
_____
_____

Daily Highlights

Sunday_____
_____
_____
_____

Monday_____
_____
_____
_____

Tuesday_____
_____
_____
_____

Wednesday_____
_____
_____
_____

Thursday_____
_____
_____
_____

Friday_____
_____
_____
_____

Saturday_____
_____
_____
_____

What I would like to remember about this week

_____
_____
_____
_____
_____
_____
_____
_____

Say something positive

Daily Highlights

Sunday_____

_____

_____

_____

Monday_____

_____

_____

_____

Tuesday_____

_____

_____

_____

Wednesday_____

_____

_____

_____

Thursday_____

_____

_____

_____

Friday_____

_____

_____

_____

Saturday_____

_____

_____

_____

What I would like to remember about this week

_____

_____

_____

_____

_____

_____

_____

_____

Daily Highlights

_nday_____
_____
_____
_____

_onday_____
_____
_____
_____

_esday_____
_____
_____
_____

_ednesday_____
_____
_____
_____

_ursday_____
_____
_____
_____

_iday_____
_____
_____
_____

_aturday_____
_____
_____
_____

What I would like to remember about this week

_____
_____
_____
_____
_____
_____
_____

Find one thing for which you are grateful

Week Beginning: _____

Daily Highlights

Sunday_____

_____

_____

_____

Monday_____

_____

_____

_____

Tuesday_____

_____

_____

_____

Wednesday_____

_____

_____

_____

Thursday_____

_____

_____

_____

Friday_____

_____

_____

_____

Saturday_____

_____

_____

_____

What I would like to remember about this week

_____

_____

_____

_____

_____

_____

_____

Daily Highlights

Sunday_____
_____
_____
_____

Monday_____
_____
_____
_____

Tuesday_____
_____
_____
_____

Wednesday_____
_____
_____
_____

Thursday_____
_____
_____
_____

Friday_____
_____
_____
_____

Saturday_____
_____
_____
_____

What I would like to remember about this week

_____
_____
_____
_____
_____
_____
_____
_____

Daily Highlights

Sunday_____
_____
_____
_____

Monday_____
_____
_____
_____

Tuesday_____
_____
_____
_____

Wednesday_____
_____
_____
_____

Thursday_____
_____
_____
_____

Friday_____
_____
_____
_____

Saturday_____
_____
_____
_____

What I would like to remember about this week

_____
_____
_____
_____
_____
_____
_____

Think happy thoughts.

Daily Highlights

nday_____
_____
_____
_____

onday_____
_____
_____
_____

esday_____
_____
_____
_____

ednesday_____
_____
_____
_____

ursday_____
_____
_____
_____

iday_____
_____
_____
_____

aturday_____
_____
_____
_____

What I would like to remember about this week

_____
_____
_____
_____
_____
_____
_____

Week Beginning: _____

Daily Highlights

Sunday_____
_____
_____
_____

Monday_____
_____
_____
_____

Tuesday_____
_____
_____
_____

Wednesday_____
_____
_____
_____

Thursday_____
_____
_____
_____

Friday_____
_____
_____
_____

Saturday_____
_____
_____
_____

What I would like to remember about this week

_____
_____
_____
_____
_____
_____
_____
_____

Week Beginning: _____

Daily Highlights

Sunday_____
_____
_____
_____

Monday_____
_____
_____
_____

Tuesday_____
_____
_____
_____

Wednesday_____
_____
_____
_____

Thursday_____
_____
_____
_____

Friday_____
_____
_____
_____

Saturday_____
_____
_____
_____

What I would like to remember about this week

_____
_____
_____
_____
_____
_____
_____

Daily Highlights

Sunday_____
_____
_____
_____

Monday_____
_____
_____
_____

Tuesday_____
_____
_____
_____

Wednesday_____
_____
_____
_____

Thursday_____
_____
_____
_____

Friday_____
_____
_____
_____

Saturday_____
_____
_____
_____

What I would like to remember about this week

_____
_____
_____
_____
_____
_____
_____
_____

Buy yourself something nice.

Daily Highlights

Sunday_____
_____
_____
_____

Monday_____
_____
_____
_____

Tuesday_____
_____
_____
_____

Wednesday_____
_____
_____
_____

Thursday_____
_____
_____
_____

Friday_____
_____
_____
_____

Saturday_____
_____
_____
_____

What I would like to remember about this week

_____
_____
_____
_____
_____
_____
_____
_____

Week Beginning: _____

Daily Highlights

nday_____
_____
_____
_____

onday_____
_____
_____
_____

esday_____
_____
_____
_____

ednesday_____
_____
_____
_____

ursday_____
_____
_____
_____

iday_____
_____
_____
_____

aturday_____
_____
_____
_____

What I would like to remember about this week

_____
_____
_____
_____
_____
_____
_____

101

Daily Highlights

Sunday_____

_____

_____

_____

Monday_____

_____

_____

_____

Tuesday_____

_____

_____

_____

Wednesday_____

_____

_____

_____

Thursday_____

_____

_____

_____

Friday_____

_____

_____

_____

Saturday_____

_____

_____

_____

What I would like to remember about this week

_____

_____

_____

_____

_____

_____

_____

_____

Week Beginning: _____

Daily Highlights

Sunday_____
_____
_____
_____

Monday_____
_____
_____
_____

Tuesday_____
_____
_____
_____

Wednesday_____
_____
_____
_____

Thursday_____
_____
_____
_____

Friday_____
_____
_____
_____

Saturday_____
_____
_____
_____

What I would like to remember about this week

_____
_____
_____
_____
_____
_____
_____

Don't allow anyone or anything to mess-up your day.

Daily Highlights

Sunday_____
_____
_____
_____

Monday_____
_____
_____
_____

Tuesday_____
_____
_____
_____

Wednesday_____
_____
_____
_____

Thursday_____
_____
_____
_____

Friday_____
_____
_____

Saturday_____
_____
_____
_____

What I would like to remember about this week

_____
_____
_____
_____
_____
_____
_____

Daily Highlights

Sunday_____
_____
_____
_____

Monday_____
_____
_____
_____

Tuesday_____
_____
_____
_____

Wednesday_____
_____
_____
_____

Thursday_____
_____
_____
_____

Friday_____
_____
_____
_____

Saturday_____
_____
_____
_____

What I would like to remember about this week

_____
_____
_____
_____
_____
_____
_____
_____

Daily Highlights

nday_____
_____
_____
_____

onday_____
_____
_____
_____

esday_____
_____
_____
_____

ednesday_____
_____
_____
_____

ursday_____
_____
_____
_____

iday_____
_____
_____
_____

aturday_____
_____
_____
_____

What I would like to remember about this week

_____
_____
_____
_____
_____
_____
_____
_____

Daily Highlights

Sunday_____

_____

_____

_____

Monday_____

_____

_____

_____

Tuesday_____

_____

_____

_____

Wednesday_____

_____

_____

_____

Thursday_____

_____

_____

_____

Friday_____

_____

_____

_____

Saturday_____

_____

_____

_____

What I would like to remember about this week

_____

_____

_____

_____

_____

_____

_____

_____

Daily Highlights

Sunday_____

_____

_____

_____

Monday_____

_____

_____

_____

Tuesday_____

_____

_____

_____

Wednesday_____

_____

_____

_____

Thursday_____

_____

_____

_____

Friday_____

_____

_____

_____

Saturday_____

_____

_____

_____

What I would like to remember about this week

_____

_____

_____

_____

_____

_____

_____

Feel good about yourself.

Week Beginning: _____

Daily Highlights

Sunday_____
_____
_____
_____

Monday_____
_____
_____
_____

Tuesday_____
_____
_____
_____

Wednesday_____
_____
_____
_____

Thursday_____
_____
_____
_____

Friday_____
_____
_____
_____

Saturday_____
_____
_____
_____

What I would like to remember about this week

_____
_____
_____
_____
_____
_____
_____
_____

Daily Highlights

Sunday_____
_____
_____
_____

Monday_____
_____
_____
_____

Tuesday_____
_____
_____
_____

Wednesday_____
_____
_____
_____

Thursday_____
_____
_____
_____

Friday_____
_____
_____
_____

Saturday_____
_____
_____
_____

What I would like to remember about this week

_____
_____
_____
_____
_____
_____
_____
_____

Daily Highlights

nday_____
_____
_____
_____

onday_____
_____
_____
_____

esday_____
_____
_____
_____

ednesday_____
_____
_____
_____

ursday_____
_____
_____
_____

iday_____
_____
_____
_____

aturday_____
_____
_____
_____

What I would like to remember about this week

_____
_____
_____
_____
_____
_____
_____

Think of someone who could use some cheering up

Call him/her

Chat for at least 5 minutes.

End with something nice.

Daily Highlights

Sunday_____

_____

_____

_____

Monday_____

_____

_____

_____

Tuesday_____

_____

_____

_____

Wednesday_____

_____

_____

_____

Thursday_____

_____

_____

_____

Friday_____

_____

_____

_____

Saturday_____

_____

_____

What I would like to remember about this week

_____

_____

_____

_____

_____

_____

_____

_____

Week Beginning: _____

Daily Highlights

Sunday_____
_____
_____
_____

Monday_____
_____
_____
_____

Tuesday_____
_____
_____
_____

Wednesday_____
_____
_____
_____

Thursday_____
_____
_____
_____

Friday_____
_____
_____
_____

Saturday_____
_____
_____
_____

What I would like to remember about this week

_____
_____
_____
_____
_____
_____
_____
_____

Smile.

Week Beginning: _____

Daily Highlights

Sunday_____
_____
_____
_____

Monday_____
_____
_____
_____

Tuesday_____
_____
_____
_____

Wednesday_____
_____
_____
_____

Thursday_____
_____
_____
_____

Friday_____
_____
_____
_____

Saturday_____
_____
_____
_____

What I would like to remember about this week

_____
_____
_____
_____
_____
_____
_____

Week Beginning: _____

Daily Highlights

nday_____
_____
_____
_____

onday_____
_____
_____
_____

esday_____
_____
_____
_____

ednesday_____
_____
_____
_____

ursday_____
_____
_____
_____

iday_____
_____
_____
_____

aturday_____
_____
_____
_____

What I would like to remember about this week

_____
_____
_____
_____
_____
_____
_____
_____

Take a few deep breaths.

In through your nose. Hold it. Out through
your mouth.

Daily Highlights

Sunday_____

_____

_____

_____

Monday_____

_____

_____

_____

Tuesday_____

_____

_____

_____

Wednesday_____

_____

_____

_____

Thursday_____

_____

_____

_____

Friday_____

_____

_____

_____

Saturday_____

_____

_____

_____

What I would like to remember about this week

_____

_____

_____

_____

_____

_____

_____

Daily Highlights

Sunday_____
_____
_____
_____

Monday_____
_____
_____
_____

Tuesday_____
_____
_____
_____

Wednesday_____
_____
_____
_____

Thursday_____
_____
_____
_____

Friday_____
_____
_____
_____

Saturday_____
_____
_____
_____

What I would like to remember about this week

_____
_____
_____
_____
_____
_____
_____
_____

Week Beginning: _____

Daily Highlights

Sunday_____
_____
_____
_____

Monday_____
_____
_____
_____

Tuesday_____
_____
_____
_____

Wednesday_____
_____
_____
_____

Thursday_____
_____
_____
_____

Friday_____
_____
_____

Saturday_____
_____
_____

What I would like to remember about this week

_____
_____
_____
_____
_____
_____
_____

Help someone in need

Daily Highlights

nday_____
_____
_____
_____

onday_____
_____
_____
_____

esday_____
_____
_____
_____

ednesday_____
_____
_____
_____

ursday_____
_____
_____
_____

iday_____
_____
_____
_____

aturday_____
_____
_____
_____

What I would like to remember about this week

_____
_____
_____
_____
_____
_____
_____

Daily Highlights

Sunday_____
_____
_____
_____

Monday_____
_____
_____
_____

Tuesday_____
_____
_____
_____

Wednesday_____
_____
_____
_____

Thursday_____
_____
_____
_____

Friday_____
_____
_____
_____

Saturday_____
_____
_____
_____

What I would like to remember about this week

_____
_____
_____
_____
_____
_____
_____
_____

Surprise someone by doing something nice for him/her

Daily Highlights

Sunday_____
_____
_____
_____

Monday_____
_____
_____
_____

Tuesday_____
_____
_____
_____

Wednesday_____
_____
_____
_____

Thursday_____
_____
_____
_____

Friday_____
_____
_____
_____

Saturday_____
_____
_____
_____

What I would like to remember about this week

_____
_____
_____
_____
_____
_____
_____
_____

Accept yourself – just the way you are.

Week Beginning: _____

Daily Highlights

Sunday_____

_____

_____

_____

Monday_____

_____

_____

_____

Tuesday_____

_____

_____

_____

Wednesday_____

_____

_____

_____

Thursday_____

_____

_____

_____

Friday_____

_____

_____

_____

Saturday_____

_____

_____

_____

What I would like to remember about this week

_____

_____

_____

_____

_____

_____

_____

_____

Week Beginning: _____

Daily Highlights

nday_____
_____
_____
_____

onday_____
_____
_____
_____

esday_____
_____
_____
_____

ednesday_____
_____
_____
_____

ursday_____
_____
_____
_____

iday_____
_____
_____
_____

aturday_____
_____
_____
_____

What I would like to remember about this week

_____
_____
_____
_____
_____
_____
_____

Daily Highlights

Sunday_____
_____
_____
_____

Monday_____
_____
_____
_____

Tuesday_____
_____
_____
_____

Wednesday_____
_____
_____
_____

Thursday_____
_____
_____
_____

Friday_____
_____
_____
_____

Saturday_____
_____
_____
_____

What I would like to remember about this week

_____
_____
_____
_____
_____
_____
_____

Greet a stranger

Daily Highlights

Sunday_____
_____
_____
_____

Monday_____
_____
_____
_____

Tuesday_____
_____
_____
_____

Wednesday_____
_____
_____
_____

Thursday_____
_____
_____
_____

Friday_____
_____
_____
_____

Saturday_____
_____
_____
_____

What I would like to remember about this week

_____
_____
_____
_____
_____
_____
_____
_____

Week Beginning: _____

Daily Highlights

Sunday_____
_____
_____
_____

Monday_____
_____
_____
_____

Tuesday_____
_____
_____
_____

Wednesday_____
_____
_____
_____

Thursday_____
_____
_____
_____

Friday_____
_____
_____
_____

Saturday_____
_____
_____
_____

What I would like to remember about this week

_____
_____
_____
_____
_____
_____
_____

Daily Highlights

Sunday_____

_____

_____

_____

Monday_____

_____

_____

_____

Tuesday_____

_____

_____

_____

Wednesday_____

_____

_____

_____

Thursday_____

_____

_____

_____

Friday_____

_____

_____

_____

Saturday_____

_____

_____

_____

What I would like to remember about this week

_____

_____

_____

_____

_____

_____

_____

_____

Say something funny to someone

Daily Highlights

Sunday_____

_____

_____

_____

Monday_____

_____

_____

_____

Tuesday_____

_____

_____

_____

Wednesday_____

_____

_____

_____

Thursday_____

_____

_____

_____

Friday_____

_____

_____

_____

Saturday_____

_____

_____

_____

What I would like to remember about this week

_____

_____

_____

_____

_____

_____

_____

_____

Daily Highlights

Sunday_____

_____

_____

_____

Monday_____

_____

_____

_____

Tuesday_____

_____

_____

_____

Wednesday_____

_____

_____

_____

Thursday_____

_____

_____

_____

Friday_____

_____

_____

_____

Saturday_____

_____

_____

_____

What I would like to remember about this week

_____

_____

_____

_____

_____

_____

_____

Daily Highlights

Sunday_____
_____
_____
_____

Monday_____
_____
_____
_____

Tuesday_____
_____
_____
_____

Wednesday_____
_____
_____
_____

Thursday_____
_____
_____
_____

Friday_____
_____
_____
_____

Saturday_____
_____
_____
_____

What I would like to remember about this week

_____
_____
_____
_____
_____
_____
_____
_____

Daily Highlights

Sunday_____
_____
_____
_____

Monday_____
_____
_____
_____

Tuesday_____
_____
_____
_____

Wednesday_____
_____
_____
_____

Thursday_____
_____
_____
_____

Friday_____
_____
_____
_____

Saturday_____
_____
_____
_____

What I would like to remember about this week

_____
_____
_____
_____
_____
_____
_____

Tell someone something you like about him/he

Daily Highlights

nday_____

_____

_____

_____

onday_____

_____

_____

_____

esday_____

_____

_____

_____

ednesday_____

_____

_____

_____

ursday_____

_____

_____

_____

iday_____

_____

_____

_____

aturday_____

_____

_____

_____

What I would like to remember about this week

_____

_____

_____

_____

_____

_____

_____

_____

Daily Highlights

Sunday_____
_____
_____
_____

Monday_____
_____
_____
_____

Tuesday_____
_____
_____
_____

Wednesday_____
_____
_____
_____

Thursday_____
_____
_____
_____

Friday_____
_____
_____
_____

Saturday_____
_____
_____
_____

What I would like to remember about this week

_____
_____
_____
_____
_____
_____
_____
_____

Week Beginning: _____

Daily Highlights

Sunday_____

_____

_____

_____

Monday_____

_____

_____

_____

Tuesday_____

_____

_____

_____

Wednesday_____

_____

_____

_____

Thursday_____

_____

_____

_____

Friday_____

_____

_____

_____

Saturday_____

_____

_____

What I would like to remember about this week

_____

_____

_____

_____

_____

_____

_____

_____

Daily Highlights

Sunday_____
_____
_____
_____

Monday_____
_____
_____
_____

Tuesday_____
_____
_____
_____

Wednesday_____
_____
_____
_____

Thursday_____
_____
_____
_____

Friday_____
_____
_____
_____

Saturday_____
_____
_____
_____

What I would like to remember about this week

_____
_____
_____
_____
_____
_____
_____
_____

Think of a happy memory.

Call someone and share it with him/her.

Week Beginning: _____

Daily Highlights

Sunday_____
_____
_____
_____

Monday_____
_____
_____
_____

Tuesday_____
_____
_____
_____

Wednesday_____
_____
_____
_____

Thursday_____
_____
_____
_____

Friday_____
_____
_____
_____

Saturday_____
_____
_____
_____

What I would like to remember about this week

_____
_____
_____
_____
_____
_____
_____
_____

Week Beginning: _____

Daily Highlights

Sunday_____

_____

_____

_____

Monday_____

_____

_____

_____

Tuesday_____

_____

_____

_____

Wednesday_____

_____

_____

_____

Thursday_____

_____

_____

_____

Friday_____

_____

_____

Saturday_____

_____

_____

What I would like to remember about this week

_____

_____

_____

_____

_____

_____

_____

Daily Highlights

Sunday_____

_____

_____

_____

Monday_____

_____

_____

_____

Tuesday_____

_____

_____

_____

Wednesday_____

_____

_____

_____

Thursday_____

_____

_____

_____

Friday_____

_____

_____

_____

Saturday_____

_____

_____

_____

What I would like to remember about this week

_____

_____

_____

_____

_____

_____

_____

_____

Week Beginning: _____

Daily Highlights

Sunday_____
_____
_____
_____

Monday_____
_____
_____
_____

Tuesday_____
_____
_____
_____

Wednesday_____
_____
_____
_____

Thursday_____
_____
_____
_____

Friday_____
_____
_____

Saturday_____
_____
_____
_____

What I would like to remember about this week

_____
_____
_____
_____
_____
_____
_____

Give away something that you like

Daily Highlights

Sunday_____

_____

_____

_____

Monday_____

_____

_____

_____

Tuesday_____

_____

_____

_____

Wednesday_____

_____

_____

_____

Thursday_____

_____

_____

_____

Friday_____

_____

_____

_____

Saturday_____

_____

_____

_____

What I would like to remember about this week

_____

_____

_____

_____

_____

_____

_____

_____

Daily Highlights

Sunday_____
_____
_____
_____

Monday_____
_____
_____
_____

Tuesday_____
_____
_____
_____

Wednesday_____
_____
_____
_____

Thursday_____
_____
_____
_____

Friday_____
_____
_____
_____

Saturday_____
_____
_____
_____

What I would like to remember about this week

_____
_____
_____
_____
_____
_____
_____
_____

Week Beginning: _____

Daily Highlights

nday_____
_____
_____
_____

onday_____
_____
_____
_____

esday_____
_____
_____
_____

ednesday_____
_____
_____
_____

ursday_____
_____
_____
_____

iday_____
_____
_____

aturday_____
_____
_____

What I would like to remember about this week

_____
_____
_____
_____
_____
_____
_____

Daily Highlights

Sunday_____

_____

_____

_____

Monday_____

_____

_____

_____

Tuesday_____

_____

_____

_____

Wednesday_____

_____

_____

_____

Thursday_____

_____

_____

_____

Friday_____

_____

_____

_____

Saturday_____

_____

_____

_____

What I would like to remember about this week

_____

_____

_____

_____

_____

_____

_____

_____

Volunteer for any cause

Daily Highlights

Sunday_____

_____

_____

_____

Monday_____

_____

_____

_____

Tuesday_____

_____

_____

_____

Wednesday_____

_____

_____

_____

Thursday_____

_____

_____

_____

Friday_____

_____

_____

_____

Saturday_____

_____

_____

_____

What I would like to remember about this week

_____

_____

_____

_____

_____

_____

_____

_____

Daily Highlights

Sunday_____
_____
_____
_____

Monday_____
_____
_____
_____

Tuesday_____
_____
_____
_____

Wednesday_____
_____
_____
_____

Thursday_____
_____
_____
_____

Friday_____
_____
_____

Saturday_____
_____
_____

What I would like to remember about this week

_____
_____
_____
_____
_____
_____
_____
_____

Daily Highlights

Sunday_____
_____
_____
_____

Monday_____
_____
_____
_____

Tuesday_____
_____
_____
_____

Wednesday_____
_____
_____
_____

Thursday_____
_____
_____
_____

Friday_____
_____
_____
_____

Saturday_____
_____
_____
_____

What I would like to remember about this week

_____
_____
_____
_____
_____
_____
_____
_____

Week Beginning: _____

Daily Highlights

nday_____

_____
_____
_____

onday_____

_____
_____
_____

esday_____

_____
_____
_____

ednesday_____

_____
_____
_____

ursday_____

_____
_____
_____

iday_____

_____
_____
_____

aturday_____

_____
_____
_____

What I would like to remember about this week

_____
_____
_____
_____
_____
_____
_____
_____

Daily Highlights

Sunday_____

_____

_____

_____

Monday_____

_____

_____

_____

Tuesday_____

_____

_____

_____

Wednesday_____

_____

_____

_____

Thursday_____

_____

_____

_____

Friday_____

_____

_____

_____

Saturday_____

_____

_____

_____

What I would like to remember about this week

_____

_____

_____

_____

_____

_____

_____

_____

Call someone who you haven't spoken to in a while.

Chat for at least 15 minutes.

Daily Highlights

Sunday_____
_____
_____
_____

Monday_____
_____
_____
_____

Tuesday_____
_____
_____
_____

Wednesday_____
_____
_____
_____

Thursday_____
_____
_____
_____

Friday_____
_____
_____
_____

Saturday_____
_____
_____
_____

What I would like to remember about this week

_____
_____
_____
_____
_____
_____
_____

Daily Highlights

Sunday_____

_____

_____

_____

Monday_____

_____

_____

_____

Tuesday_____

_____

_____

_____

Wednesday_____

_____

_____

_____

Thursday_____

_____

_____

_____

Friday_____

_____

_____

_____

Saturday_____

_____

_____

_____

What I would like to remember about this week

_____

_____

_____

_____

_____

_____

_____

Daily Highlights

Sunday_____
_____
_____
_____

Monday_____
_____
_____
_____

Tuesday_____
_____
_____
_____

Wednesday_____
_____
_____
_____

Thursday_____
_____
_____
_____

Friday_____
_____
_____
_____

Saturday_____
_____
_____
_____

What I would like to remember about this week

_____
_____
_____
_____
_____
_____
_____
_____

Close your eyes.

Allow yourself to be...

Just be - for about half-an-hour.

Daily Highlights

Sunday_____

_____

_____

_____

Monday_____

_____

_____

_____

Tuesday_____

_____

_____

_____

Wednesday_____

_____

_____

_____

Thursday_____

_____

_____

_____

Friday_____

_____

_____

_____

Saturday_____

_____

_____

_____

What I would like to remember about this week

_____

_____

_____

_____

_____

_____

_____

_____

Week Beginning: _____

Daily Highlights

Sunday_____
_____
_____
_____

Monday_____
_____
_____
_____

Tuesday_____
_____
_____
_____

Wednesday_____
_____
_____
_____

Thursday_____
_____
_____
_____

Friday_____
_____
_____
_____

Saturday_____
_____
_____
_____

What I would like to remember about this week

_____
_____
_____
_____
_____
_____
_____
_____

Daily Highlights

Sunday_____
_____
_____
_____

Monday_____
_____
_____
_____

Tuesday_____
_____
_____
_____

Wednesday_____
_____
_____
_____

Thursday_____
_____
_____
_____

Friday_____
_____
_____
_____

Saturday_____
_____
_____
_____

What I would like to remember about this week

_____
_____
_____
_____
_____
_____
_____
_____

Week Beginning: _____

Daily Highlights

Sunday_____

_____

_____

_____

Monday_____

_____

_____

_____

Tuesday_____

_____

_____

_____

Wednesday_____

_____

_____

_____

Thursday_____

_____

_____

_____

Friday_____

_____

_____

_____

Saturday_____

_____

_____

_____

What I would like to remember about this week

_____

_____

_____

_____

_____

_____

_____

_____

Eat with someone new today

Week Beginning: _____

Daily Highlights

nday_____

_____

_____

_____

onday_____

_____

_____

_____

esday_____

_____

_____

_____

ednesday_____

_____

_____

_____

ursday_____

_____

_____

_____

iday_____

_____

_____

_____

aturday_____

_____

_____

_____

What I would like to remember about this week

_____

_____

_____

_____

_____

_____

_____

_____

Daily Highlights

Sunday_____

_____

_____

_____

Monday_____

_____

_____

_____

Tuesday_____

_____

_____

_____

Wednesday_____

_____

_____

_____

Thursday_____

_____

_____

_____

Friday_____

_____

_____

_____

Saturday_____

_____

_____

_____

What I would like to remember about this week

_____

_____

_____

_____

_____

_____

_____

_____

Daily Highlights

Sunday_____
_____
_____
_____

Monday_____
_____
_____
_____

Tuesday_____
_____
_____
_____

Wednesday_____
_____
_____
_____

Thursday_____
_____
_____
_____

Friday_____
_____
_____

Saturday_____
_____
_____

What I would like to remember about this week

_____
_____
_____
_____
_____
_____
_____
_____

Identify something for which you are grateful

Week Beginning: _____

Daily Highlights

Sunday_____
_____
_____
_____

Monday_____
_____
_____
_____

Tuesday_____
_____
_____
_____

Wednesday_____
_____
_____
_____

Thursday_____
_____
_____
_____

Friday_____
_____
_____
_____

Saturday_____
_____
_____

What I would like to remember about this week

_____
_____
_____
_____
_____
_____
_____
_____

Week Beginning: _____

Daily Highlights

Sunday_____

_____

_____

_____

Monday_____

_____

_____

_____

Tuesday_____

_____

_____

_____

Wednesday_____

_____

_____

_____

Thursday_____

_____

_____

_____

Friday_____

_____

_____

_____

Saturday_____

_____

_____

_____

What I would like to remember about this week

_____

_____

_____

_____

_____

_____

_____

Week Beginning: _____

Daily Highlights

Sunday_____
_____
_____
_____

Monday_____
_____
_____
_____

Tuesday_____
_____
_____
_____

Wednesday_____
_____
_____
_____

Thursday_____
_____
_____
_____

Friday_____
_____
_____
_____

Saturday_____
_____
_____

What I would like to remember about this week

_____
_____
_____
_____
_____
_____
_____
_____

Daily Highlights

Sunday_____

_____

_____

_____

Monday_____

_____

_____

_____

Tuesday_____

_____

_____

_____

Wednesday_____

_____

_____

_____

Thursday_____

_____

_____

_____

Friday_____

_____

_____

_____

Saturday_____

_____

_____

_____

What I would like to remember about this week

_____

_____

_____

_____

_____

_____

_____

Daily Highlights

Sunday_____
_____
_____
_____

Monday_____
_____
_____
_____

Tuesday_____
_____
_____
_____

Wednesday_____
_____
_____
_____

Thursday_____
_____
_____
_____

Friday_____
_____
_____
_____

Saturday_____
_____
_____
_____

What I would like to remember about this week

_____
_____
_____
_____
_____
_____
_____

Tell someone thanks for being a friend

Daily Highlights

Sunday_____
_____
_____
_____

Monday_____
_____
_____
_____

Tuesday_____
_____
_____
_____

Wednesday_____
_____
_____
_____

Thursday_____
_____
_____
_____

Friday_____
_____
_____
_____

Saturday_____
_____
_____
_____

What I would like to remember about this week

_____
_____
_____
_____
_____
_____
_____
_____

Week Beginning: _____

Daily Highlights

Sunday_____
_____
_____
_____

Monday_____
_____
_____
_____

Tuesday_____
_____
_____
_____

Wednesday_____
_____
_____
_____

Thursday_____
_____
_____
_____

Friday_____
_____
_____
_____

Saturday_____
_____
_____
_____

What I would like to remember about this week

_____
_____
_____
_____
_____
_____
_____
_____

Daily Highlights

nday_____
_____
_____
_____

onday_____
_____
_____
_____

esday_____
_____
_____
_____

ednesday_____
_____
_____
_____

ursday_____
_____
_____
_____

riday_____
_____
_____
_____

aturday_____
_____
_____
_____

What I would like to remember about this week

_____
_____
_____
_____
_____
_____

Week Beginning: _____

Daily Highlights

Sunday_____

_____

_____

_____

Monday_____

_____

_____

_____

Tuesday_____

_____

_____

_____

Wednesday_____

_____

_____

_____

Thursday_____

_____

_____

_____

Friday_____

_____

_____

_____

Saturday_____

_____

_____

_____

What I would like to remember about this week

_____

_____

_____

_____

_____

_____

_____

_____

Be humble

Daily Highlights

Sunday_____
_____
_____
_____

Monday_____
_____
_____
_____

Tuesday_____
_____
_____
_____

Wednesday_____
_____
_____
_____

Thursday_____
_____
_____
_____

Friday_____
_____
_____
_____

Saturday_____
_____
_____
_____

What I would like to remember about this week

_____
_____
_____
_____
_____
_____
_____
_____

Week Beginning: _____

Daily Highlights

Sunday_____
_____
_____
_____

Monday_____
_____
_____
_____

Tuesday_____
_____
_____
_____

Wednesday_____
_____
_____
_____

Thursday_____
_____
_____
_____

Friday_____
_____
_____

Saturday_____
_____
_____
_____

What I would like to remember about this week

_____
_____
_____
_____
_____
_____
_____
_____

Sometimes you are much better off alone.

Be comfortable in your own skin.

Learn to enjoy your own company.

Daily Highlights

nday_____
_____
_____
_____

onday_____
_____
_____
_____

esday_____
_____
_____
_____

ednesday_____
_____
_____
_____

ursday_____
_____
_____
_____

iday_____
_____
_____
_____

aturday_____
_____
_____

What I would like to remember about this week

_____
_____
_____
_____
_____
_____
_____
_____

Daily Highlights

Sunday_____

_____

_____

_____

Monday_____

_____

_____

_____

Tuesday_____

_____

_____

_____

Wednesday_____

_____

_____

_____

Thursday_____

_____

_____

_____

Friday_____

_____

_____

_____

Saturday_____

_____

_____

_____

What I would like to remember about this week

_____

_____

_____

_____

_____

_____

_____

_____

Remember to wear your seatbelt

Week Beginning: _____

Daily Highlights

Sunday_____
_____
_____
_____

Monday_____
_____
_____
_____

Tuesday_____
_____
_____
_____

Wednesday_____
_____
_____
_____

Thursday_____
_____
_____
_____

Friday_____
_____
_____
_____

Saturday_____
_____
_____
_____

What I would like to remember about this week

_____
_____
_____
_____
_____
_____
_____
_____

Week Beginning: _____

Daily Highlights

Sunday_____
_____
_____
_____

Monday_____
_____
_____
_____

Tuesday_____
_____
_____
_____

Wednesday_____
_____
_____
_____

Thursday_____
_____
_____
_____

Friday_____
_____
_____
_____

Saturday_____
_____
_____

What I would like to remember about this week

_____
_____
_____
_____
_____
_____
_____
_____

Daily Highlights

Sunday_____
_____
_____
_____

Monday_____
_____
_____
_____

Tuesday_____
_____
_____
_____

Wednesday_____
_____
_____
_____

Thursday_____
_____
_____
_____

Friday_____
_____
_____
_____

Saturday_____
_____
_____
_____

What I would like to remember about this week

_____
_____
_____
_____
_____
_____
_____

Daily Highlights

Sunday _____
_____
_____
_____

Monday _____
_____
_____
_____

Tuesday _____
_____
_____
_____

Wednesday _____
_____
_____
_____

Thursday _____
_____
_____
_____

Friday _____
_____
_____

Saturday _____
_____
_____
_____

What I would like to remember about this week

_____
_____
_____
_____
_____
_____
_____

Remember to turn off the phone while you drive.

It can wait – no matter what it is.

Week Beginning: _____

Daily Highlights

Sunday_____
_____
_____
_____

Monday_____
_____
_____
_____

Tuesday_____
_____
_____
_____

Wednesday_____
_____
_____
_____

Thursday_____
_____
_____
_____

Friday_____
_____
_____

Saturday_____
_____
_____

What I would like to remember about this week

_____
_____
_____
_____
_____
_____
_____

Daily Highlights

Sunday_____

_____

_____

_____

Monday_____

_____

_____

_____

Tuesday_____

_____

_____

_____

Wednesday_____

_____

_____

_____

Thursday_____

_____

_____

_____

Friday_____

_____

_____

_____

Saturday_____

_____

_____

_____

What I would like to remember about this week

_____

_____

_____

_____

_____

_____

_____

_____

Week Beginning: _____

Daily Highlights

Sunday_____
_____
_____
_____

Monday_____
_____
_____
_____

Tuesday_____
_____
_____
_____

Wednesday_____
_____
_____
_____

Thursday_____
_____
_____
_____

Friday_____
_____
_____
_____

Saturday_____
_____
_____
_____

What I would like to remember about this week

_____
_____
_____
_____
_____
_____
_____
_____

You don't always have to win.

Week Beginning: _____

Daily Highlights

Sunday_____
_____
_____
_____

Monday_____
_____
_____
_____

Tuesday_____
_____
_____
_____

Wednesday_____
_____
_____
_____

Thursday_____
_____
_____
_____

Friday_____
_____
_____
_____

Saturday_____
_____
_____

What I would like to remember about this week

_____
_____
_____
_____
_____
_____
_____

Week Beginning: _____

Daily Highlights

Sunday_____
_____
_____
_____

Monday_____
_____
_____
_____

Tuesday_____
_____
_____
_____

Wednesday_____
_____
_____
_____

Thursday_____
_____
_____
_____

Friday_____
_____
_____
_____

Saturday_____
_____
_____
_____

What I would like to remember about this week

_____
_____
_____
_____
_____
_____
_____
_____

Week Beginning: _____

Daily Highlights

Sunday_____
_____
_____
_____

Monday_____
_____
_____
_____

Tuesday_____
_____
_____
_____

Wednesday_____
_____
_____
_____

Thursday_____
_____
_____
_____

Friday_____
_____
_____
_____

Saturday_____
_____
_____
_____

What I would like to remember about this week

_____
_____
_____
_____
_____
_____
_____
_____

Daily Highlights

Sunday_____

_____
_____
_____

Monday_____

_____
_____
_____

Tuesday_____

_____
_____
_____

Wednesday_____

_____
_____
_____

Thursday_____

_____
_____
_____

Friday_____

_____
_____
_____

Saturday_____

_____
_____
_____

What I would like to remember about this week

_____
_____
_____
_____
_____
_____
_____
_____

Daily Highlights

Sunday_____
_____
_____
_____

Monday_____
_____
_____
_____

Tuesday_____
_____
_____
_____

Wednesday_____
_____
_____
_____

Thursday_____
_____
_____
_____

Friday_____
_____
_____
_____

Saturday_____
_____
_____

What I would like to remember about this week

_____
_____
_____
_____
_____
_____
_____
_____

Daily Highlights

Sunday_____
_____
_____
_____

Monday_____
_____
_____
_____

Tuesday_____
_____
_____
_____

Wednesday_____
_____
_____
_____

Thursday_____
_____
_____
_____

Friday_____
_____
_____
_____

Saturday_____
_____
_____
_____

What I would like to remember about this week

_____
_____
_____
_____
_____
_____
_____

Sometimes it's okay to say "no."

Daily Highlights

Sunday_____
_____
_____
_____

Monday_____
_____
_____
_____

Tuesday_____
_____
_____
_____

Wednesday_____
_____
_____
_____

Thursday_____
_____
_____
_____

Friday_____
_____
_____
_____

Saturday_____
_____
_____
_____

What I would like to remember about this week

_____
_____
_____
_____
_____
_____
_____

Week Beginning: _____

Daily Highlights

Sunday_____
_____
_____
_____

Monday_____
_____
_____
_____

Tuesday_____
_____
_____
_____

Wednesday_____
_____
_____
_____

Thursday_____
_____
_____
_____

Friday_____
_____
_____
_____

Saturday_____
_____
_____
_____

What I would like to remember about this week

_____
_____
_____
_____
_____
_____
_____
_____

Daily Highlights

Sunday_____

_____

_____

_____

Monday_____

_____

_____

_____

Tuesday_____

_____

_____

_____

Wednesday_____

_____

_____

_____

Thursday_____

_____

_____

_____

Friday_____

_____

_____

_____

Saturday_____

_____

_____

_____

What I would like to remember about this week

_____

_____

_____

_____

_____

_____

_____

_____

Week Beginning: _____

Daily Highlights

Sunday_____
_____
_____
_____

Monday_____
_____
_____
_____

Tuesday_____
_____
_____
_____

Wednesday_____
_____
_____
_____

Thursday_____
_____
_____
_____

Friday_____
_____
_____

Saturday_____
_____
_____
_____

What I would like to remember about this week

_____
_____
_____
_____
_____
_____
_____
_____

213

Daily Highlights

Sunday_____

_____

_____

_____

Monday_____

_____

_____

_____

Tuesday_____

_____

_____

_____

Wednesday_____

_____

_____

_____

Thursday_____

_____

_____

_____

Friday_____

_____

_____

_____

Saturday_____

_____

_____

_____

What I would like to remember about this week

_____

_____

_____

_____

_____

_____

_____

Week Beginning: _____

Daily Highlights

Sunday_____
_____
_____
_____

Monday_____
_____
_____
_____

Tuesday_____
_____
_____
_____

Wednesday_____
_____
_____
_____

Thursday_____
_____
_____
_____

Friday_____
_____
_____
_____

Saturday_____
_____
_____

What I would like to remember about this week

_____
_____
_____
_____
_____
_____
_____
_____

Daily Highlights

Sunday_____

_____

_____

_____

Monday_____

_____

_____

_____

Tuesday_____

_____

_____

_____

Wednesday_____

_____

_____

_____

Thursday_____

_____

_____

_____

Friday_____

_____

_____

_____

Saturday_____

_____

_____

_____

What I would like to remember about this week

_____

_____

_____

_____

_____

_____

_____

_____

Week Beginning: _____

Daily Highlights

Sunday_____

_____

_____

_____

Monday_____

_____

_____

_____

Tuesday_____

_____

_____

_____

Wednesday_____

_____

_____

_____

Thursday_____

_____

_____

_____

Friday_____

_____

_____

_____

Saturday_____

_____

_____

What I would like to remember about this week

_____

_____

_____

_____

_____

_____

_____

_____

Don't do things that hurt other people.

Week Beginning: _____

Daily Highlights

Sunday_____

_____
_____
_____

Monday_____

_____
_____
_____

Tuesday_____

_____
_____
_____

Wednesday_____

_____
_____
_____

Thursday_____

_____
_____
_____

Friday_____

_____
_____
_____

Saturday_____

_____
_____
_____

What I would like to remember about this week

_____
_____
_____
_____
_____
_____
_____
_____

Daily Highlights

Sunday_____
_____
_____
_____

Monday_____
_____
_____
_____

Tuesday_____
_____
_____
_____

Wednesday_____
_____
_____
_____

Thursday_____
_____
_____
_____

Friday_____
_____
_____
_____

Saturday_____
_____
_____
_____

What I would like to remember about this week

_____
_____
_____
_____
_____
_____
_____

Week Beginning: _____

Daily Highlights

ꞏnday_____

_____

_____

_____

onday_____

_____

_____

_____

ꞏesday_____

_____

_____

_____

ꞏednesday_____

_____

_____

_____

ꞏursday_____

_____

_____

_____

ꞏiday_____

_____

_____

aturday_____

_____

_____

What I would like to remember about this week

_____

_____

_____

_____

_____

_____

_____

Week Beginning: _____

Daily Highlights

Sunday_____
_____
_____
_____

Monday_____
_____
_____
_____

Tuesday_____
_____
_____
_____

Wednesday_____
_____
_____
_____

Thursday_____
_____
_____
_____

Friday_____
_____
_____
_____

Saturday_____
_____
_____
_____

What I would like to remember about this week

_____
_____
_____
_____
_____
_____
_____
_____

Week Beginning: _____

Daily Highlights

Sunday_____
_____
_____
_____

Monday_____
_____
_____
_____

Tuesday_____
_____
_____
_____

Wednesday_____
_____
_____
_____

Thursday_____
_____
_____
_____

Friday_____
_____
_____
_____

Saturday_____
_____
_____

What I would like to remember about this week

_____
_____
_____
_____
_____
_____
_____

Respect yourself.

Respect others.

Week Beginning: _____

Daily Highlights

Sunday_____

_____

_____

_____

Monday_____

_____

_____

_____

Tuesday_____

_____

_____

_____

Wednesday_____

_____

_____

_____

Thursday_____

_____

_____

_____

Friday_____

_____

_____

_____

Saturday_____

_____

_____

_____

What I would like to remember about this week

_____

_____

_____

_____

_____

_____

_____

_____

Daily Highlights

Sunday_____

_____

_____

_____

Monday_____

_____

_____

_____

Tuesday_____

_____

_____

_____

Wednesday_____

_____

_____

_____

Thursday_____

_____

_____

_____

Friday_____

_____

_____

_____

Saturday_____

_____

_____

_____

What I would like to remember about this week

_____

_____

_____

_____

_____

_____

_____

_____

Others may not understand you.

That's okay.

Week Beginning: _____

Daily Highlights

Sunday_____
_____
_____
_____

Monday_____
_____
_____
_____

Tuesday_____
_____
_____
_____

Wednesday_____
_____
_____
_____

Thursday_____
_____
_____
_____

Friday_____
_____
_____
_____

Saturday_____
_____
_____
_____

What I would like to remember about this week

_____
_____
_____
_____
_____
_____
_____
_____

Week Beginning: _____

Daily Highlights

Sunday_____
_____
_____
_____

Monday_____
_____
_____
_____

Tuesday_____
_____
_____
_____

Wednesday_____
_____
_____
_____

Thursday_____
_____
_____
_____

Friday_____
_____
_____

Saturday_____
_____
_____

What I would like to remember about this week

_____
_____
_____
_____
_____
_____
_____

Daily Highlights

Sunday_____
_____
_____
_____

Monday_____
_____
_____
_____

Tuesday_____
_____
_____
_____

Wednesday_____
_____
_____
_____

Thursday_____
_____
_____
_____

Friday_____
_____
_____
_____

Saturday_____
_____
_____
_____

What I would like to remember about this week

_____
_____
_____
_____
_____
_____
_____
_____

What you do matters – especially when you are alone.

Week Beginning: _____

Daily Highlights

Sunday_____
_____
_____
_____

Monday_____
_____
_____
_____

Tuesday_____
_____
_____
_____

Wednesday_____
_____
_____
_____

Thursday_____
_____
_____
_____

Friday_____
_____
_____
_____

Saturday_____
_____
_____
_____

What I would like to remember about this week

_____
_____
_____
_____
_____
_____
_____

Daily Highlights

nday_____

_____

_____

_____

onday_____

_____

_____

_____

esday_____

_____

_____

_____

ednesday_____

_____

_____

_____

ursday_____

_____

_____

_____

iday_____

_____

_____

_____

aturday_____

_____

_____

_____

What I would like to remember about this week

_____

_____

_____

_____

_____

_____

_____

_____

Daily Highlights

Sunday_____

_____

_____

_____

Monday_____

_____

_____

_____

Tuesday_____

_____

_____

_____

Wednesday_____

_____

_____

_____

Thursday_____

_____

_____

_____

Friday_____

_____

_____

_____

Saturday_____

_____

_____

_____

What I would like to remember about this week

_____

_____

_____

_____

_____

_____

_____

_____

Week Beginning: _____

Daily Highlights

Sunday_____
_____
_____
_____

Monday_____
_____
_____
_____

Tuesday_____
_____
_____
_____

Wednesday_____
_____
_____
_____

Thursday_____
_____
_____
_____

Friday_____
_____
_____
_____

Saturday_____
_____
_____
_____

What I would like to remember about this week

_____
_____
_____
_____
_____
_____
_____

Daily Highlights

Sunday_____

_____

_____

_____

Monday_____

_____

_____

_____

Tuesday_____

_____

_____

_____

Wednesday_____

_____

_____

_____

Thursday_____

_____

_____

_____

Friday_____

_____

_____

_____

Saturday_____

_____

_____

_____

What I would like to remember about this week

_____

_____

_____

_____

_____

_____

_____

_____

Week Beginning: _____

Daily Highlights

Sunday_____

_____

_____

_____

Monday_____

_____

_____

_____

Tuesday_____

_____

_____

_____

Wednesday_____

_____

_____

_____

Thursday_____

_____

_____

_____

Friday_____

_____

_____

_____

Saturday_____

_____

_____

_____

What I would like to remember about this week

_____

_____

_____

_____

_____

_____

_____

Daily Highlights

Sunday_____
_____
_____
_____

Monday_____
_____
_____
_____

Tuesday_____
_____
_____
_____

Wednesday_____
_____
_____
_____

Thursday_____
_____
_____
_____

Friday_____
_____
_____
_____

Saturday_____
_____
_____
_____

What I would like to remember about this week

_____
_____
_____
_____
_____
_____
_____
_____

**Your words should mean something –
especially to you.**

Daily Highlights

Sunday_____
_____
_____
_____

Monday_____
_____
_____
_____

Tuesday_____
_____
_____
_____

Wednesday_____
_____
_____
_____

Thursday_____
_____
_____
_____

Friday_____
_____
_____
_____

Saturday_____
_____
_____
_____

What I would like to remember about this week

_____
_____
_____
_____
_____
_____
_____
_____

Daily Highlights

Sunday_____
_____
_____
_____

Monday_____
_____
_____
_____

Tuesday_____
_____
_____
_____

Wednesday_____
_____
_____
_____

Thursday_____
_____
_____
_____

Friday_____
_____
_____
_____

Saturday_____
_____
_____

What I would like to remember about this week

_____
_____
_____
_____
_____
_____
_____
_____

Daily Highlights

Sunday_____
_____
_____
_____

Monday_____
_____
_____
_____

Tuesday_____
_____
_____
_____

Wednesday_____
_____
_____
_____

Thursday_____
_____
_____
_____

Friday_____
_____
_____
_____

Saturday_____
_____
_____
_____

What I would like to remember about this week

_____
_____
_____
_____
_____
_____
_____
_____

Daily Highlights

Sunday_____
_____
_____
_____

Monday_____
_____
_____
_____

Tuesday_____
_____
_____
_____

Wednesday_____
_____
_____
_____

Thursday_____
_____
_____
_____

Friday_____
_____
_____
_____

Saturday_____
_____
_____

What I would like to remember about this week

_____
_____
_____
_____
_____
_____
_____
_____

Daily Highlights

Sunday_____

_____

_____

_____

Monday_____

_____

_____

_____

Tuesday_____

_____

_____

_____

Wednesday_____

_____

_____

_____

Thursday_____

_____

_____

_____

Friday_____

_____

_____

_____

Saturday_____

_____

_____

_____

What I would like to remember about this week

_____

_____

_____

_____

_____

_____

_____

_____

Be true to yourself.

Daily Highlights

Sunday_____
_____
_____
_____

Monday_____
_____
_____
_____

Tuesday_____
_____
_____
_____

Wednesday_____
_____
_____
_____

Thursday_____
_____
_____
_____

Friday_____
_____
_____
_____

Saturday_____
_____
_____
_____

What I would like to remember about this week

_____
_____
_____
_____
_____
_____
_____
_____

Daily Highlights

_nday_____
_____
_____
_____

_onday_____
_____
_____
_____

_esday_____
_____
_____
_____

_ednesday_____
_____
_____
_____

_ursday_____
_____
_____
_____

_iday_____
_____
_____

_aturday_____
_____
_____

What I would like to remember about this week

_____
_____
_____
_____
_____
_____
_____

Week Beginning: _____

Daily Highlights

Sunday_____
_____
_____
_____

Monday_____
_____
_____
_____

Tuesday_____
_____
_____
_____

Wednesday_____
_____
_____
_____

Thursday_____
_____
_____
_____

Friday_____
_____
_____
_____

Saturday_____
_____
_____
_____

What I would like to remember about this week

_____
_____
_____
_____
_____
_____
_____
_____

Week Beginning: _____

Daily Highlights

Sunday_____

_____

_____

_____

Monday_____

_____

_____

_____

Tuesday_____

_____

_____

_____

Wednesday_____

_____

_____

_____

Thursday_____

_____

_____

_____

Friday_____

_____

_____

_____

Saturday_____

_____

_____

_____

What I would like to remember about this week

_____

_____

_____

_____

_____

_____

_____

_____

Keep the past behind you

Week Beginning: _____

Daily Highlights

Sunday_____
_____
_____
_____

Monday_____
_____
_____
_____

Tuesday_____
_____
_____
_____

Wednesday_____
_____
_____
_____

Thursday_____
_____
_____
_____

Friday_____
_____
_____

Saturday_____
_____
_____

What I would like to remember about this week

_____
_____
_____
_____
_____
_____
_____
_____

Daily Highlights

Sunday_____
_____
_____
_____

Monday_____
_____
_____
_____

Tuesday_____
_____
_____
_____

Wednesday_____
_____
_____
_____

Thursday_____
_____
_____
_____

Friday_____
_____
_____
_____

Saturday_____
_____
_____
_____

What I would like to remember about this week

_____
_____
_____
_____
_____
_____
_____
_____

Week Beginning: _____

Daily Highlights

Sunday_____
_____
_____
_____

Monday_____
_____
_____
_____

Tuesday_____
_____
_____
_____

Wednesday_____
_____
_____
_____

Thursday_____
_____
_____
_____

Friday_____
_____
_____
_____

Saturday_____
_____
_____
_____

What I would like to remember about this week

_____
_____
_____
_____
_____
_____
_____
_____

Daily Highlights

Sunday_____

_____

_____

_____

Monday_____

_____

_____

_____

Tuesday_____

_____

_____

_____

Wednesday_____

_____

_____

_____

Thursday_____

_____

_____

_____

Friday_____

_____

_____

_____

Saturday_____

_____

_____

_____

What I would like to remember about this week

_____

_____

_____

_____

_____

_____

_____

_____

Be realistic

Week Beginning: _____

Daily Highlights

Sunday_____
_____
_____
_____

Monday_____
_____
_____
_____

Tuesday_____
_____
_____
_____

Wednesday_____
_____
_____
_____

Thursday_____
_____
_____
_____

Friday_____
_____
_____
_____

Saturday_____
_____
_____
_____

What I would like to remember about this week

_____
_____
_____
_____
_____
_____
_____

Week Beginning: _____

Daily Highlights

Sunday_____
_____
_____
_____

Monday_____
_____
_____
_____

Tuesday_____
_____
_____
_____

Wednesday_____
_____
_____
_____

Thursday_____
_____
_____
_____

Friday_____
_____
_____

Saturday_____
_____
_____
_____

What I would like to remember about this week

_____
_____
_____
_____
_____
_____
_____

Daily Highlights

Sunday_____

_____

_____

_____

Monday_____

_____

_____

_____

Tuesday_____

_____

_____

_____

Wednesday_____

_____

_____

_____

Thursday_____

_____

_____

_____

Friday_____

_____

_____

_____

Saturday_____

_____

_____

_____

What I would like to remember about this week

_____

_____

_____

_____

_____

_____

_____

_____

Week Beginning: _____

Daily Highlights

Sunday _____
_____
_____
_____

Monday _____
_____
_____
_____

Tuesday _____
_____
_____
_____

Wednesday _____
_____
_____
_____

Thursday _____
_____
_____
_____

Friday _____
_____
_____
_____

Saturday _____
_____
_____
_____

What I would like to remember about this week

_____
_____
_____
_____
_____
_____
_____

Daily Highlights

Sunday_____
_____
_____
_____

Monday_____
_____
_____
_____

Tuesday_____
_____
_____
_____

Wednesday_____
_____
_____
_____

Thursday_____
_____
_____
_____

Friday_____
_____
_____
_____

Saturday_____
_____
_____
_____

What I would like to remember about this week

_____
_____
_____
_____
_____
_____
_____
_____

Week Beginning: _____

Daily Highlights

Sunday_____
_____
_____
_____

Monday_____
_____
_____
_____

Tuesday_____
_____
_____
_____

Wednesday_____
_____
_____
_____

Thursday_____
_____
_____
_____

Friday_____
_____
_____
_____

Saturday_____
_____
_____
_____

What I would like to remember about this week

_____
_____
_____
_____
_____
_____
_____
_____

Daily Highlights

Sunday_____

_____

_____

_____

Monday_____

_____

_____

_____

Tuesday_____

_____

_____

_____

Wednesday_____

_____

_____

_____

Thursday_____

_____

_____

_____

Friday_____

_____

_____

_____

Saturday_____

_____

_____

_____

What I would like to remember about this week

_____

_____

_____

_____

_____

_____

_____

_____

Week Beginning: _____

Daily Highlights

Sunday_____
_____
_____
_____

Monday_____
_____
_____
_____

Tuesday_____
_____
_____
_____

Wednesday_____
_____
_____
_____

Thursday_____
_____
_____
_____

Friday_____
_____
_____
_____

Saturday_____
_____
_____

What I would like to remember about this week

_____
_____
_____
_____
_____
_____
_____

Be yourself.

Week Beginning: _____

Daily Highlights

nday_____
_____
_____
_____

onday_____
_____
_____
_____

esday_____
_____
_____
_____

ednesday_____
_____
_____
_____

ursday_____
_____
_____
_____

iday_____
_____
_____
_____

aturday_____
_____
_____
_____

What I would like to remember about this week

_____
_____
_____
_____
_____
_____
_____

Daily Highlights

Sunday_____

_____

_____

_____

Monday_____

_____

_____

_____

Tuesday_____

_____

_____

_____

Wednesday_____

_____

_____

_____

Thursday_____

_____

_____

_____

Friday_____

_____

_____

_____

Saturday_____

_____

_____

_____

What I would like to remember about this week

_____

_____

_____

_____

_____

_____

_____

_____

Week Beginning: _____

Daily Highlights

Sunday_____

_____

_____

_____

Monday_____

_____

_____

_____

Tuesday_____

_____

_____

_____

Wednesday_____

_____

_____

_____

Thursday_____

_____

_____

_____

Friday_____

_____

_____

_____

Saturday_____

_____

_____

_____

What I would like to remember about this week

_____

_____

_____

_____

_____

_____

_____

_____

Week Beginning: _____

Daily Highlights

Sunday_____
_____
_____
_____

Monday_____
_____
_____
_____

Tuesday_____
_____
_____
_____

Wednesday_____
_____
_____
_____

Thursday_____
_____
_____
_____

Friday_____
_____
_____
_____

Saturday_____
_____
_____
_____

What I would like to remember about this week

_____
_____
_____
_____
_____
_____
_____

You won't be right all the time.

Acknowledge when you are wrong.

Apologize and move on.

Daily Highlights

Sunday_____
_____
_____
_____

Monday_____
_____
_____
_____

Tuesday_____
_____
_____
_____

Wednesday_____
_____
_____
_____

Thursday_____
_____
_____
_____

Friday_____
_____
_____
_____

Saturday_____
_____
_____
_____

What I would like to remember about this week

_____
_____
_____
_____
_____
_____
_____
_____

Daily Highlights

Sunday _____
_____
_____
_____

Monday _____
_____
_____
_____

Tuesday _____
_____
_____
_____

Wednesday _____
_____
_____
_____

Thursday _____
_____
_____
_____

Friday _____
_____
_____
_____

Saturday _____
_____
_____
_____

What I would like to remember about this week

_____
_____
_____
_____
_____
_____
_____

Week Beginning: _____

Daily Highlights

Sunday_____
_____
_____
_____

Monday_____
_____
_____
_____

Tuesday_____
_____
_____
_____

Wednesday_____
_____
_____
_____

Thursday_____
_____
_____
_____

Friday_____
_____
_____
_____

Saturday_____
_____
_____
_____

What I would like to remember about this week

_____
_____
_____
_____
_____
_____
_____
_____

You are unique.

Just as unique as everyone else is.

Daily Highlights

Sunday_____

_____

_____

_____

Monday_____

_____

_____

_____

Tuesday_____

_____

_____

_____

Wednesday_____

_____

_____

_____

Thursday_____

_____

_____

_____

Friday_____

_____

_____

_____

Saturday_____

_____

_____

_____

What I would like to remember about this week

_____

_____

_____

_____

_____

_____

_____

_____

Week Beginning: _____

Daily Highlights

Sunday_____
_____
_____
_____

Monday_____
_____
_____
_____

Tuesday_____
_____
_____
_____

Wednesday_____
_____
_____
_____

Thursday_____
_____
_____
_____

Friday_____
_____
_____
_____

Saturday_____
_____
_____
_____

What I would like to remember about this week

_____
_____
_____
_____
_____
_____
_____

Daily Highlights

Sunday_____

_____

_____

_____

Monday_____

_____

_____

_____

Tuesday_____

_____

_____

_____

Wednesday_____

_____

_____

_____

Thursday_____

_____

_____

_____

Friday_____

_____

_____

_____

Saturday_____

_____

_____

_____

What I would like to remember about this week

_____

_____

_____

_____

_____

_____

_____

_____

Week Beginning: _____

Daily Highlights

nday_____
_____
_____
_____

onday_____
_____
_____
_____

esday_____
_____
_____
_____

ednesday_____
_____
_____
_____

ursday_____
_____
_____
_____

iday_____
_____
_____
_____

aturday_____
_____
_____
_____

What I would like to remember about this week

_____
_____
_____
_____
_____
_____
_____
_____

Set daily goals.

Important Contacts

Name:

_____

Tel #:

_____

E-mail:

_____

Name:

_____

Tel#: _____

E-mail:

_____

Name:

_____

Tel#: _____

E-mail:

_____

Name:

_____

Tel#: _____

E-mail:

_____

Important Contacts

ame:

_____

el #:

_____

-mail:

_____

ame:

_____

el#: _____

-mail:

_____

ame:

_____

el#: _____

-mail:

_____

ame:

_____

el#: _____

-mail:

_____

Important Contacts

Name:

_____

Tel #:

_____

E-mail:

_____

Name:

_____

Tel#: _____

E-mail:

_____

Name:

_____

Tel#: _____

E-mail:

_____

Name:

_____

Tel#: _____

E-mail:

_____

Important Contacts

Name:

_____

Tel #:

_____

E-mail:

_____

Name:

_____

Tel#: _____

E-mail:

_____

Name:

_____

Tel#: _____

E-mail:

_____

Name:

_____

Tel#: _____

E-mail:

_____

283

Important Contacts

Name:

_____

Tel #:

_____

E-mail:

_____

Name:

_____

Tel#: _____

E-mail:

_____

Name:

_____

Tel#: _____

E-mail:

_____

Name:

_____

Tel#: _____

E-mail:

_____

Important Contacts

Name:

_____

Tel #:

_____

E-mail:

_____

Name:

_____

Tel#:

_____

E-mail:

_____

Name:

_____

Tel#:

_____

E-mail:

_____

Name:

_____

Tel#:

_____

E-mail:

_____

Important Contacts

Name:

_____

Tel #:

_____

E-mail:

_____

Name:

_____

Tel#: _____

E-mail:

_____

Name:

_____

Tel#: _____

E-mail:

_____

Name:

_____

Tel#: _____

E-mail:

_____

Important Contacts

Name:

_____

Tel #:

_____

E-mail:

_____

Name:

_____

Tel#: _____

E-mail:

_____

Name:

_____

Tel#:_____

E-mail:

_____

Name:

_____

Tel#: _____

E-mail:

_____

Important Contacts

Name:

_____

Tel #:

_____

E-mail:

_____

Name:

_____

Tel#: _____

E-mail:

_____

Name:

_____

Tel#:_____

E-mail:

_____

Name:

_____

Tel#: _____

E-mail:

_____

Important Contacts

ame:

_____

el #:

_____

mail:

_____

ame:

_____

el#: _____

mail:

_____

ame:

_____

el#:_____

mail:

_____

ame:

_____

el#: _____

mail:

_____

Notes

Notes

Notes

Notes

Notes

Other Important Information

Other Important Information

Other Important Information

Find peace within.